CW00693134

COTSWOLD
PANORAMAS

STEPHEN DOREY

MYRIAD
LONDON

First published in 2009 by Myriad Books Limited
35 Bishopsthorpe Road, London SE26 4PA

ISBN 1 84746 266 9
EAN 978 1 84746 266 4

Designed by Jerry Goldie Graphic Design

Printed in China

www.myriadbooks.com

Previous page: Duntisbourne Leer
This page: Autumn mist receding from the Cotswold scarp at Prinknash

CONTENTS

Around Cheltenham & Gloucester 4

Around Cirencester 22

North Cotswolds 36

South Cotswolds 62

East Cotswolds 76

Around Stroud 86

AROUND CHELTENHAM AND GLOUCESTER

The beautiful town of Cheltenham and the county town of Gloucester are situated to the west of the Cotswolds. A large escarpment dominates the countryside, looking out over the river Severn and its tributaries. Cheltenham developed as a spa and resort to rival nearby Bath, while Gloucester's growth was linked to its role as a port in the 19th century.

1 CHELTENHAM 6
2 CLEEVE COMMON 8
3 HAILES 10
4 TEMPLE GUITING 12
5 NAUNTON 14
6 SEVENHAMPTON 16
7 BRIMPSFIELD 18
8 GLOUCESTER DOCKS 20

OPPOSITE – CHELTENHAM

Pittville Pump Room in Pittville Park, Cheltenham was completed in 1830 during the town's heyday as a spa.

This elegant spa town retains an air of Georgian grandeur, a legacy of the Regency period when it was a fashionable place to take the waters. The discovery of a spring in 1761, in what is now Cheltenham Ladies' College, gave rise to a sudden burst of popularity and affluence and the spa at Cheltenham soon began to rival Bath in its splendour. Much of the architecture and layout of today's town dates from this period.

CLEEVE COMMON

Just to the north-east of Cheltenham, Cleeve Hill and Cleeve Common are a broad expanse of open countryside which give magnificent views over the Severn Vale and the Malvern Hills. Here can be found West Down which, at 1082ft (330m) is the highest point in the Cotswolds. Cleeve Common was an important grazing area during the Middle Ages and an earthwork known as the Ring shows that the Romans kept livestock here.

This tranquil wooded pastureland, just two miles from Winchcombe, is the site of a ruined Cistercian abbey founded by Richard, Earl of Cornwall, brother of Henry III in 1246. Around 1270 the abbey acquired a phial said to contain the blood of Christ and Hailes became a major centre of pilgrimage. It was so popular that an inn, now on the site of the former George Hotel at Winchcombe, was built to house pilgrims.

TEMPLE GUITING

Situated on the river Windrush, not far from its sister village of Guiting Power, Temple Guiting is dominated by the medieval St Mary's church, which stands on high ground at the south end of the village. The view from the churchyard is considered to be one of the most idyllic in the Cotswolds. The church interior boasts an elaborate set of wooden panels over the south door representing the Ten Commandments.

NAUNTON

This straggling village in the upper Windrush valley has long been a centre for sheep rearing, ever since the valley became monastic land in the Middle Ages. Naunton's other industry was the production of stone roofing slates. At one time 30,000 slates a week were dug from thin stone seams in nearby mines. Naunton boasts a picturesque dovecote, erected in 1660.

SEVENHAMPTON

This parish was first recorded in 1086 indicating seven small settlements within the area. The village lies at the top of the valley of the infant river Coln (which in 1537 was called Senhampton Brook) and is surrounded by farmland. The church is of Norman origin and the 16th century manor house was occupied by the Lawrence family from 1550 to 1890.

BRIMPSFIELD

This pretty village lies at a height of 800ft overlooking the headwaters of the river Frome. William the Conqueror gave the manor to William Giffard, and his family built a castle there. His descendant, John Giffard, rebelled against Edward II and was executed in 1322. The castle was destroyed and its site can still be seen beside the pathway to the church.

GLOUCESTER DOCKS

Opened in 1827, Gloucester Docks gave direct access to seagoing ships via the Severn estuary. From here goods were transferred to canal barges for transportation throughout the Midlands. The old warehouses, many now transformed into flats, make this a popular location for filming period drama; fans of *The Onedin Line* will find the Biddle's warehouse familiar.

HORTON CHEMIST
STRADLINGS

AROUND CIRENCESTER

Circencester was an important city during the Roman era and stood at the junction of three major roads: the Fosse Way, the Ermin Way and Akeman Street. In the Middle Ages the town was a centre for the wool trade and today it is a busy market town and an important cross-roads in the southern Cotswolds.

1 BIBURY 24

2 COLN ROGERS 26

3 YANWORTH 28

4 RENDCOMB 30

5 DUNTISBOURNE ABBOTS 32

6 DUNTISBOURNE LEER 34

OPPOSITE – ST JOHN THE BAPTIST, CIRENCESTER

The beautiful parish church of St John the Baptist is one of the largest churches in England.

BIBURY

The gorgeous village of Bibury has its origins in Saxon times, but the bulk of the village dates from the Middle Ages. These pretty cottages are on the opposite side of the river from the picturesque Arlington Row, a terrace of weavers' cottages built to house workers from Arlington Mill at the other end of the village. In the 1870s William Morris, the artist and writer, declared that Bibury was the most beautiful village in England.

COLN ROGERS

The village of Coln Rogers takes its name from the river on which it stands; it is situated at the point where the river starts to broaden on its way south from the high Cotswolds to the flatter lands below. On either side of the valley there are fine woodlands and pleasant walks. Inside the church of St Andrew a beautiful plaque commemorates the fact that Coln Rogers is a "thankful village" – all the men from the village who saw action in the First World War returned home alive.

YANWORTH

The delightful village of Yanworth is on the Macmillan Way footpath and makes a good starting point for walks to Chedworth to the south-west or Hampnett to the north-east. Its Norman church stands slightly outside the village amongst a group of farm buildings. The church, which is open daily, has much beautiful decorative Norman work on the outside and the interior boasts a 16th century wall painting of a scythe-bearing Father Time.

RENDCOMB

The handsome estate village of Rendcomb was built to serve Rendcomb Court, a mansion built in the 19th century – today it is a boarding school. The parish church of St Peter contains a carved 12th century font. This was created between 1130-40 and shows the 12 Apostles; 11 are identifiable by symbols but the twelfth, representing Judas, is blank with only a pair of feet showing. Only Hereford cathedral can boast a comparable font.

DUNTISBOURNE ABBOTS

This small village, originally owned by the abbots of Gloucester, is situated in the valley of the river Dunt. The village church of St Peter dates from the 12th century but is built on the site of an earlier Saxon church. Access to the churchyard is through a picturesque lych-gate. The Hoar Stone long barrow, a prehistoric chambered tomb set on a long mound, can be found about a mile to the south of the village.

DUNTISBOURNE LEER

Like its close neighbour Duntisbourne Leer takes its name from the abbey that once owned it – in this case Lire abbey in Normandy. Today the hamlet consists of two farmhouses and outbuildings grouped around a shallow ford over the river Dunt. In the 19th century a number of Dissenters took up residence in the two villages. One of them, Elizabeth Cross, later set up a mission school on the Pacific island of Tonga. The King and Queen of Tonga remain Methodists to the present day.

NORTH COTSWOLDS

This high escarpment overlooks the Vale of Evesham to the west. It contains the market towns of Stow-on-the-Wold and Chipping Camden, famous in the Middle Ages for their wool and cattle markets. The beautiful village of Broadway developed as a stagecoach route from east to west and is regarded by many as the classic Cotswold town.

1 STOW-ON-THE-WOLD 38
2 LOWER SLAUGHTER 40
3 UPPER SLAUGHTER 42
4 MORETON-IN-MARSH 44
5 CHIPPING CAMPDEN 46
6 SAINTBURY 48
7 WILLERSEY 50
8 BROADWAY 52
9 BROADWAY TOWER 54
10 SNOWSHILL 56
11 SNOWSHILL CHURCHYARD 58
12 STANWAY 60

OPPOSITE – SAINTBURY

Ranged along the side of Saintbury Hill, this beautiful village has fine views over the Vale of Evesham.

M.S.GUM M.R.Pharm.S.
STOW PHARMACY
CONCORDE
FILM
£4.49
THE TALBOT
FINE FOOD
Shelley's
KU56 DHA

The highest town in the Cotswolds, the shape of the town's market square is partly dictated by the need for stall holders to be protected from the wind. The town is located on the top of a hill between the valleys of the rivers Evenlode and the Dikler. The beautiful parish church of St Edward was built between the 11th and the 15th centuries. Its tower is 88 ft high and houses the highest set of bells in Gloucestershire.

LOWER SLAUGHTER

The beautiful villages of Upper and Lower Slaughter are situated on the river Eye, known locally as Slaughter Brook. Several footbridges span the river and a footpath links Lower Slaughter with Upper Slaughter. At one end of Lower Slaughter a large mill pond feeds a working water wheel. The 19th century mill – the Old Mill – is open to the public and houses a museum. St Mary's church and the village hall are both late Victorian while the manor house dates back to 1650.

UPPER SLAUGHTER

Although the name sounds bloodthirsty, the name "Slaughter" probably derives from the old English word "Slohtre" meaning slough or boggy place. Standing on a hillside above the river Eye, the village is grouped around a small square. Completely belying its name, Upper Slaughter is a "double thankful village" – all the men it sent to fight in the First and Second World Wars returned home alive.

MORETON-IN-MARSH

Located on the Fosse Way, Moreton has long been a travellers' town. Its many elegant inns and hotels date back to the days of the stagecoach when the town was a stop on the London to Worcester route. In 1853 the Oxford to Worcester railway arrived. Every Tuesday is market day, with popular stalls straggling along the wide high street. In the centre of the street is the Redesdale Hall – a covered market erected in 1887 by the Mitford family.

CHIPPING CAMPDEN

Chipping Campden developed as a market town serving the wool and cattle trade and the many fine buildings that it boasts are evidence of its successful past. Built in 1627, the market hall was intended for the sale of cheese, butter and poultry when the wool trade began to decline. The town has a variety of beautiful buildings which date from different periods; the use of golden Cotswold stone gives Chipping Campden a great sense of unity, from the sturdy arches of the market hall to the lofty pinnacles of the church.

SAINTBURY

The classic Cotswold village of Saintbury is located close to both Chipping Campden and Broadway. From the top of Saintbury Hill there are beautiful views north over the Vale of Evesham. The elegant spire of the church of St Nicholas is seen here rising above the treeline. The church is famous for its peal of six bells and its Sheela-na-gig – a Celtic fertility goddess.

WILLERSEY

With its spacious village green, duck pond and ancient church, Willersey is a typical English village, one of four lying at the foot of the north-west escarpment between Broadway and Meon Hill. The annual Willersey wake, held towards the end of June on the village green, is a central feature of village life. Willersey has two historic pubs – the magnificent 17th century Bell Inn, overlooking the duckpond, and the New Inn on Main Street.

BROADWAY

The village of Broadway was once an important stop for stagecoaches on the London to Worcester route. A new turnpike road was opened in 1736 and at one time seven coaches passed through the village every day. Many of the fine buildings along Broadway's main street began as inns to serve the passing trade. With the coming of the railways the coach trade faded but Broadway had its own station and it quickly became a stopping off point for exploration of the Cotswolds.

BROADWAY TOWER

One mile south-east of the village of Broadway, the tower is one of England's best viewpoints – on a clear day it is possible to see 13 counties and enjoy views of the Vale of Evesham, the Vale of Gloucester, the Severn valley and the Welsh mountains. At one time Broadway Tower was owned by William Morris and was virtually a country retreat for the pre-Raphaelites. It is said to have been the inspiration for the tower of Amon Hen and the Hill of Seeing in *The Lord of the Rings* by JRR Tolkien.

SNOWSHILL

Three miles south of Broadway, Snowshill was owned by Winchcombe Abbey from 821 until the Dissolution of the Monasteries. In 1919 the almost derelict manor house was bought and restored by Charles Paget Wade who needed somewhere to display his wonderful collection of arts and crafts from different countries. In collaboration with the architect M H Baillie-Scott he designed the garden and laid out its terraces and ponds between 1920-23. Snowshill Manor was donated to the National Trust in 1951.

SNOWSHILL CHURCHYARD

Typical Cotswold stone cottages surround the sloping churchyard in the centre of Snowshill. The church of St Barnabas dates from 1864, replacing an earlier building. Next to the church sits the historic Snowshill Arms and a small gateway to its right leads to Snowshill Manor. This Tudor mansion houses the collection of Charles Paget Wade who spent a lifetime assembling a stunning collection of craftsmanship from around the world.

STANWAY

The small village of Stanway is dominated by the gateway to Stanway House. Built during the 1580s on the site of an earlier manor house, it is mostly Jacobean in style and has a remarkable 60-pane full-height bay window. Opposite the drive to Stanway House is a thatched cricket pavilion. This was a gift to the village by J M Barrie, author of *Peter Pan*, a frequent visitor to the area in the early years of the 20th century.

SOUTH COTSWOLDS

The World Heritage city of Bath is at the southernmost extremity of the Cotswolds. To the north-east lies the Cotswold escarpment, dotted with pretty villages such as Hawkesbury and Cold Ashton. Nearby Castle Combe is claimed by many to be one of the prettiest villages in England.

1 BATH 64

2 COLD ASHTON 66

3 CASTLE COMBE 68

4 HAWKESBURY 70

5 WESTONBIRT 72

6 TETBURY 74

OPPOSITE – BATH

The Romans named Bath *Aquae Sulis* and made use of the natural hot springs to indulge their passion for bathing.

During the Middle Ages Bath was largely in royal and monastic hands. It was not until after the Civil War that the city became a health resort for the aristocracy. The new Bath was largely built in the Classical style with long stretches of identical facades which give the impression of palatial scale and classical decorum.

COLD ASHTON

Situated on the southern edge of the Cotswolds, Cold Ashton derives its name from the winds that sweep in over the Bristol Channel. Cold Ashton Manor dates from the Jacobean period and was probably erected by John Gunning, a former mayor of Bristol in 1629.

CASTLE COMBE

Castle Combe is centred on a market cross that reflects its growth through wool trading. The village stands on the By Brook and there is a charming bridge that spans the stream. In 1966 this section of the brook was converted into a miniature port complete with jetty and boats for the filming of *Dr Dolittle*. There are many fine walks in the area and the village is on the Macmillan Way long-distance footpath.

HAWKESBURY

Nestling in a wooded coombe below the Cotswold scarp, Hawkesbury is dominated by its parish church which dates back to the 12th century. On the edge of the village is the Somerset Monument. The slightly tapering tower is approximately 100 ft (30m high) and is a local well-known landmark. It was erected in1846 to commemorate General Lord Edward Somerset who served at Waterloo and died in 1842.

The glorious Westonbirt Arboretum covers an area of 600 acres and includes an area of ancient semi-natural woodland. This magnificent collection of trees and shrubs was established in 1829 by the Holford family and today it is one of two national tree collections maintained by the Forestry Commission. Open to the public, its 17 miles of paths give access to many rare plants. It is hoped that Westonbirt will one day house the world's best collection of maples.

TETBURY

Situated between Cirencester and Bath close to the Fosse Way, Tetbury developed into an important market town. Its 17th century market house is an imposing building which used to be even higher but was reduced by one storey in 1817. Tetbury's original courthouse now houses a Police Museum which tells the story of the Gloucestershire Police Constabulary since its founding in 1839.

EAST COTSWOLDS

For many visitors travelling west this area is the "gateway" to the Cotswolds. It contains many beautiful market towns including Burford, a famous stagecoach route in the 18th and 19th centuries.

1 BOURTON-ON-THE-WATER 78

2 BURFORD 80

3 SWINBROOK 82

4 FAIRFORD 84

OPPOSITE – KEBLE'S BRIDGE, EASTLEACH MARTIN

Constructed from large flat stones, this pretty footbridge is named after the Keble family, lords of the manor of Eastleach Turville in the 16th century.

The Victoria Hall
The Mad Hatter

Situated on the river Windrush, the beautiful village of Bourton-on-the-Water is spanned by five ornamental bridges. Packed with attractions, Bourton is particularly famous for its Model Village which is a small-scale replica of the village. Other temptations include the Cotswolds Motor Museum, the Dragonfly Maze and Birdland, a bird sanctuary that includes a small colony of penguins.

BURFORD

Regarded as the eastern gateway to the Cotswolds, Burford built its reputation on wool, quarrying and coaching. In its heyday in the 18th century it was an important stop on routes to Oxford and London and the town's inns competed in offering "Burford Bait" – huge meals to attract the coaching trade. Stone from quarries near Burford was used to construct some of Britain's finest buildings including Blenheim Palace and St Paul's cathedral.

SWINBROOK

The attractive village of Swinbrook lies a few miles north-east of Burford. The church is famous for its monument to the Fettiplace family, which shows six male members of the family lying on their right-hand sides looking out into the church. The churchyard contains the grave of Nancy Mitford whose father, Lord Redesdale, built Swinbrook House. This Cotswold mansion features in her comic masterpiece, *Love in a Cold Climate*.

FAIRFORD

The beautiful village of Fairford was granted a market charter in 1135 when Henry I gave permission for a twice weekly market. The church of St Mary was built by the Tame family who became prosperous as a result of the wool industry. Other important buildings in Fairford include the 17th century Bull Hotel and Fairford Mill. The village is on the eastern edge of the Cotswold Water Park, a complex of more than 140 lakes which provide habitats for wildfowl.

AROUND STROUD

The busy market town of Stroud lies at the heart of five valleys. The hills encircling the town can be seen from almost every street. The surrounding countryside with its secret valleys and honey-coloured stone villages was made famous by Laurie Lee in his autobiographical novel *Cider With Rosie*.

1 COALEY PEAK 88

2 ELCOMBE 90

3 SLAD 92

4 PAINSWICK 94

5 MISERDEN 96

OPPOSITE – STROUD

At the height of its prosperity in the Middle Ages there were 150 cloth mills in and around Stroud. The legacy of this industry can be seen in the historic buildings in and around the town.

COALEY PEAK

Commanding wide-ranging views across the Severn Vale and the Forest of Dean, Coaley Peak consists of 12 acres of grassland on the edge of the Cotswolds escarpment. It is bordered to the south by the Frocester Hill nature reserve, and to the north-east by Stanley woods. Woodchester Park, a beautiful valley containing a "lost garden" and a chain of five lakes, owned by the National Trust, lies to the east.

ELCOMBE

Snow drapes the tiny hamlet of Elcombe which nestles in a small offshoot of the more famous Slad Valley, north-east of Stroud. Although it consists of only a few cottages (it once had a small general shop and possibly a pub) it was for 27 years the holiday home of the social reformer, R H Tawney. Near to the village, on Swift's Hill, is the Elliott nature reserve – one of the country's most important wildflower habitats.

SLAD

The small village of Slad was the childhood home of the author Laurie Lee. Life in the village in the 1920s is brilliantly evoked in his autobiography *Cider With Rosie*. The village today is remarkably unspoiled and it is still possible to gain a sense of village life as described by Lee in the 1920s. The oldest building in the village is probably Steanbridge House, an early 17th century gabled clothier's house. Some weavers' cottages also date from this period.

PAINSWICK

The stream below Painswick once provided power for its woollen mills whilst its crystal clear water made the village an important place for the dyeing of cloth. At the centre of the village is a fine church with an elegant 17th century tower. Surrounding the church are colonnades of yew trees which have been in place since 1792. Legend has it that there are only 99 trees as the devil always kills the hundredth.

MISERDEN

The pretty village of Miserden has buildings from a number of periods – the two-storey dower house dates from the 18th century while the church, which has late Saxon origins, was extensively restored in the 1880s. To the east of the village is Misarden Park, a large Elizabethan mansion with exquisite gardens. With glorious views overlooking the Golden Valley (so-called because of the wealth generated by the woollen industry) Misarden Park's gardens are open from April to September.